T0194741

ON JUPITER PLACE

BOOKS BY NICHOLAS CHRISTOPHER

POETRY

Crossing the Equator: New & Selected Poems, 1972-2004 (2004)

Atomic Field: Two Poems (2000)

The Creation of the Night Sky (1998)

5° (1995)

In the Year of the Comet (1992)

Desperate Characters: A Novella in Verse (1988)

A Short History of the Island of Butterflies (1986)

On Tour With Rita (1982)

FICTION

Tiger Rag (2013)

The Bestiary (2007)

Franklin Flyer (2002)

A Trip to the Stars (2000)

Veronica (1996)

The Soloist (1986)

NONFICTION

Somewhere in the Night: Film Noir & the American City (1997)

FOR CHILDREN

The True Adventures of Nicolò Zen (2014)

EDITOR

Walk on the Wild Side: Urban American Poetry Since 1975 (1994)

Under 35: The New Generation of American Poets (1989)

ON

JUPITER

PLACE

poems

NICHOLAS CHRISTOPHER

COUNTERPOINT
BERKELEY

Library of Congress Cataloging-in-Publication Data
Names: Christopher, Nicholas, author.
Title: On Jupiter place : poems / Nicholas Christopher.
Description: Berkely, CA : Counterpoint, 2016.
Identifiers: LCCN 2015039652 I ISBN 9781619027176 (hardcover)
Classification: LCC PS3553.H754 A6 2016 I DDC 811/.54—dc23
LC record available at http://lccn.loc.gov/2015039652

ISBN 978-1-61902-909-5

Cover design by Kelly Winton
Interior design by Megan Jones Design

COUNTERPOINT
2560 Ninth Street, Suite 318
Berkeley, CA 94710
www.counterpointpress.com

for Constance

CONTENTS

ON JUPITER PLACE

1

ON JUPITER PLACE

After my mother was diagnosed
with tuberculosis I lived
in one of the identical
brick houses on a long street
with my grandfather who worked
twelve-hour days six days a week
and my grandmother
who was too restless
to stay home for long
so that I was often left on my own
at age four with plenty of time
to meet the neighbors
Mr. Porti the building inspector
who died of a heart attack
behind the wheel of his Plymouth
and Mr. Cleary the Con Ed linesman
with the Marine Corps tattoo
who chainsmoked Camels
and his beautiful daughter Nora
the nurse in her crisp uniform
who worked the night shift
and walked home from the bus stop
every morning at eight

and his son Neal Jr. arrested

in Chinatown with a truckload

of stolen fireworks

and four doors down

Mrs. Kornstein whose husband

was gassed at Auschwitz

where she received

a different sort of tattoo

the jagged numerals on her wrist

that she refused to remove

and two doors down from her

behind a wall of evergreens

Mr. Boehringer the baker

a Bund member during the war

who spoke only German at home

and told anyone willing to listen

including his granddaughter

Heidi with her blond pigtails

that Franklin Roosevelt was a Jew

in league with Stalin —

Heidi who ate uncooked

hot dogs without buns

they tasted like bologna she said

which was what the Lazzeri twins

Vincent and Little Steve

piled on Silvercup bread

with no mustard or mayo

their father Big Steve a mobster
who every Christmas
gave his wife a fur coat
and on their tenth anniversary
a two-tone Coupe de Ville
that he washed and waxed
on Sundays in their driveway
next door to Mr. Porti's family
struggling behind drawn drapes
his daughter Genevieve
in hand-me-down dresses
and scuffed shoes was my friend
her mother the widow
had suffered a nervous breakdown
so that Genevieve too
was being raised by her grandmother
herself a widow born in Sicily
who carried a cane to ward off dogs
and across the street from them
Mr. Fallon the used car salesman
who had no license
and was driven to work
by his wife a secret drinker
that everyone knew about
both of them tormented
by their roughneck son
who one day put me

in a headlock until I turned blue
and I knocked his tooth out
and bloodied his nose
and his mother screamed that I was a savage
that we were all savages
though in fact I rarely got into trouble
and mostly kept to myself
while my father all that time
lived alone in the small apartment
that had been our home
before my mother was hospitalized
and held down two jobs
one to support us
the other to pay her medical bills
until finally she was released
from the hospital
and that first afternoon was resting
in my grandmother's room
when I was brought in to her
I hadn't seen her in a long time
she was pale and very thin
her hair was cut short
and I told her to get out
of my grandmother's bed
out of her room
I didn't know who she was anymore
maybe I never did or could —

not the girl that danced
until dawn on her wedding night
or the middle-aged woman
with ailments real and imaginary
who withered beneath
the weight of her fears —
for when she died many years later
having loved me (I know) as best she could
she was still a stranger

THE GRAVEYARD SHIFT

I work the graveyard shift in a city of believers
hunched over a steel desk in a cone of light

facing a window with drawn blinds
beyond which the innocents are being slaughtered

in an enormous courtyard against all four walls
firing squads rotating around the clock

while masked men in the watchtowers
keep count in red ink on red pads

simultaneously recording and concealing
the numbers of dead

and nodding with each round of gunfire
mumbling praise to their leader

and his god whose righteousness and mercy
he mirrors while I keep to my work

with bowed head and unblinking eyes
sorting papers affixing stamps

having long ago given up trying
to stop my ears or black out my fear

my face burning not with shame but exhaustion
for I only sleep a few hours a night

and I eat once a day
cold scrapple and rice porridge

like a prisoner myself
in a cell that requires no locks

unable to recognize my own handwriting
even when I've left myself a note

reminding me of who I once was but never
(anymore) what I might have been

which later I crumple and burn
in a standard issue ashtray

the momentary lick of flame
no more or less remote to me than a star

THE SECRET LIFE OF LOIS LANE

A woman in love with a man who is two men,
and both of them in love with her.
His "secret identity" a ruse to keep her at arm's length,
away from his more masculine self —
the iron body that would give him away.
She is a crack reporter, trained to observe
the minutest details in shifting situations,
who doesn't recognize the man she loves
when he slips on a pair of horn-rimmed glasses.
His blue-black hair, Olympic physique,
and distinctive profile suddenly obscure to her.
Flying above the jeweled city in his arms,
she kisses him passionately, yet an hour later,
working beside a fellow reporter —
a timid man in a boxy suit —
doesn't notice that the two men possess
identical voice(s), smile(s), and scent(s).
She has suspicions, intangible, inchoate,
but whenever she puts 2 + 2 together —
she of the steel-trap mind — comes up with 5.
How enormous is her denial?
And how subliminal, in her case, is the sublime?
Theirs is not a dysfunction easily categorized:

her blindness, his ambivalence, the juggling
of personas with which he dizzies her.
She fears he is stringing her along,
insisting that if his enemies learned
of their relationship, they would not hesitate
to kidnap her and blackmail him,
putting her in constant peril.
So no one must ever know.
They are the most secret of secret lovers,
each tormented by restraints
of which the other is unaware:
he in his everyman guise, playing the coward,
wants her to love him *for himself,*
rather than his alter ego,
the fearless champion, godlike avenger,
faster than a speeding bullet,
more powerful than a locomotive . . .
it's a bird, it's a plane, it's
something that was never meant to be,
so rife with pain and hopelessness
that it drives him to despair,
neutralizing his powers as no opponent can:
invulnerable, with X-ray vision,
he can time-travel, divert rivers,
pulverize asteroids, tunnel to the earth's core,
and in his bare hand compress
a chunk of coal into a ninety-carat diamond.

Yet he is unable to resolve the dilemma
of his double life and declare his love.
His secrets are familiar to us, even mundane —
pretending to be so much less than what he is,
suppressing his bizarre history —
but what of her secrets?
Beautiful, ambitious, resourceful,
who is she exactly and where did she come from?
Not an exploding planet in a distant galaxy,
an advanced civilization of which she is the lone survivor,
but some antiseptic American town
where the girls marry young and maintain
their silence through childbearing,
housekeeping, and stifled desires —
a fate she escaped through force of will,
the application of talent she was encouraged
to suppress by the mother who feared for her
and the father they both feared,
the violent drunken policeman she fled
one night on a train to the big city,
seeking refuge, hoping to find
a man of her dreams,
and when none appeared,
settling into a career,
and soon enough wanting little else,
her life finally hers alone.
She was free to travel, to take lovers —

a painter, a pilot, a ballplayer, a politician,

and once, after three martinis, another woman —

free to smoke opium in Macao

and hashish in Tangiers,

hike the Andes and kayak the Kona coast,

collect amber amulets and sharks' teeth,

join an ashram in Santa Fe

and suffer bouts of bulimia,

and after her mother's suicide

attend séances, trying to connect with her,

to explain that she too could have escaped

without putting a bullet through her brain.

And then he came along, swooping down

with the light of the universe in his veins

and a supreme destiny: to battle evil,

and save mankind from itself.

She fell hard for him, making love

on remote islets and tropical beaches,

weekends at the Arctic ice palace

he built himself in a single day,

an indefatigable lover for whom

she gave up everything but her job,

awaiting his calls, refusing other men,

growing older even as he remained young —

not a wrinkle in his brow

nor a gray hair on his head —

so that when he refused once and for all

to relent and love her openly,
offering up the same tired explanation,
To protect you from my enemies
(who could not have crushed her hopes as he did),
she began nursing a terrible anger
and desperation that deafened her
to the music of the world
until she saw no way out
except to destroy him.
And because she could get closer
to him than any other human being,
she arranged a rendezvous one night,
putting on his favorite dress,
deep blue, with a scarf to match,
and had him fly her to a mountain peak,
as he had done countless times before,
embracing and kissing him
beneath the stars from which he had come,
pulling him closer as he grew weaker,
his breath failing, eyes rolling back in his head,
so quickly that he never said a word,
accomplishing what arch-criminals,
elaborate weapons, and entire armies could not:
she killed him.
For though it was common knowledge
that the one element lethal to him
was the green mineral which had comprised

the bedrock of his birthplace,
only she, wearing a chip of it as a pendant,
could have pressed it to his chest
until his heart went cold.
After which she suffered grievously,
paralyzed by guilt, more adrift than ever,
imagining she could not feel worse
until she discovered that the shy, awkward man
who for so long had sat beside her
in the newsroom, always remembering
her birthday, sending her flowers,
trying in vain to date her,
had disappeared without a trace
on the same day the city began mourning
the Man of Steel —
shops shuttered, flags at half-staff,
schoolchildren inconsolable,
and grown men weeping in the streets.
And then she knew.
And disappeared herself, forever.

MY FATHER CROSSED THE THIRD AVENUE BRIDGE

as snow blanketed the row houses
and repair shops

the junkyards and factories
after he had spent two days

on a foldout cot
in a hospital room in the Bronx

watching his own father's vital signs
flicker and flatline on a monitor

beside the bed so that a week
after a stroke paralyzed him

whatever was left of that old man
was gone like a wisp of smoke

seeping under the door and out a window
and like the river finding its way

to the harbor and the open sea
and beyond that the sea of light

whose cresting waves like snowcapped mountains
we may glimpse in this life

on those rare occasions
when all things seem possible

A BUDDHIST MONK IN THE
BUS STATION IN PROVIDENCE

on Christmas Day 1974 awaiting
his connection in a snowstorm
said he rejected the doctrine of the *Bardo*
which insists a man is thrown into limbo
in the interval between death and rebirth
and instead believed that the latter occurs
in an instant and is nothing more
than the awakening of a stranger
who has left another stranger behind

MOCKINGBIRDS

for Constance

by the hundreds
sleep in a windswept tree
on a steep slope
their white bellies
easily mistaken for moon
blossoms or unripened fruit
until one of them
darts between branches
squabbling over a perch
to grip until dawn
when the breakers below
recede from the reefs
they were pounding
before birds alighted
on this island
and lizards scaled its cliffs
and the first men
carved spears from saplings
and fished beneath constellations
they had yet to name

THE SAILOR'S GRAVE ON THE PRAIRIE

He had traveled many miles
seeking a plot of land,
but the homesteaders
who saw him pass,
a stranger with an oar
strapped to his back,
assumed he was headed to sea,
the tall ships
with clouds for sails,
the ports rising out of mist.
In fact, he wanted a house
of stone and mortar,
wood planed from fresh timber,
tar and flashing
to seal out the wind.
No one knows
what stopped him here,
how he died
and who broke
into the hard earth
and laid him to rest,
marking the grave,

not with a cross or stone,

but his bleached oar

to which a compass

had been strung

with a bowline knot.

It may be that even

the local outlaws refrained

from taking that compass,

either because they knew

it is bad luck to steal

from the dead,

or — more likely —

because it belonged

to a man who had lost his way.

LOST NOTEBOOK

9/24/08

A door with a thousand locks
and ten thousand hinges
swings open effortlessly
onto the underworld.

9/25

On Mott Street four men
in red skullcaps
bang drums and cymbals
to root out the demons
infiltrating Bright Sun Imports
where the owner,
a cigarette between his lips,
his hand on the cashier's leg,
watches a girl on rollerskates,
singing in Mandarin,
round the corner.

9/26

In a tenement
a vine climbs the pocked wall
from a window box

to the window above
where it flowers
for a woman who depends
on the stranger below
to water it.

9/27

Through a steel door
ajar on Baxter Street
a Buddhist priest
in a yellow robe
has placed a circle of candles
around a girl in a wheelchair.

9/28

A bald child
nearly transparent
in the sunlight
leaves the hospital
on crutches,
his mother guiding him
through traffic
to a bus stop.
Eight years ago today,
my own mother died in that hospital.

9/29

As the stock market crashes,
monitors in Times Square
flash numerals that the crazies
scramble on their calculators,
seeking a formula for acquiring riches
in calamitous times,
encoded by Rameses II,
deciphered by Sufis,
preserved by Freemasons.
Cults spring up
around the notion
that the formula is microscopically inscribed,
but forever unreadable,
on every coin in the world
including the ones in your pocket.

9/30

A palimpsest seven miles up,
among blue clouds,
a ghost plane
like the one I saw
from a remote island
a week before 9/11.

10/1

In what was once called
Red China
the Yellow River
carried thousands of refugees
to the Yellow Sea,
among them a girl on Pell Street
chewing Red Hots
and scooping ice cream
from dusk to dawn
beneath a poster
of Mars that glows.

10/5

A quartz wall
through which the world is distorted
and over which
no person sane or otherwise
would want to climb
even if he could.

10/9

At nightfall a chalice spills
in the ikon over the door
of the Ukranian church
and a stream of light,

like lava, pours
from a dark cloud.

10/13

Penitents in a circle
hold mirrors to the sun,
blinding one another,
while a flautist on the radio
plays an ancient Greek scale.

10/15

A black cigarette burning down
in a white ashtray.
When the music ends,
a woman who never put it to her lips
stubs it out.

10/23

Its flowers — red, pink, green,
and in Manhattan yellow —
can be dried and pestled
to flavor soup and color cheese.
Its three slow syllables
claim many derivations:
Mary-gould, Marygold, Mary gowles,
Mariguild, Marry-gold…

Mary's flowers,
Mary mother of Jesus
golden in the sun.

10/25

Gusts knocking people off balance
on side streets.
A dog barking at the wind.

10/30

Is it easier to accept déjà vu as a moment
out of another life (the true definition)
rather than a moment in
our current life recalled unexpectedly?
How many people in this city
are asking themselves this question at 4 A.M.?

11/3

A great stillness on Election Eve.
The vast continent.
Its millions of souls
between two oceans.
And in a small room
on a television the weather report
for a single county:
cool and clear.

11/12

Flying into Madrid before dawn.
Iron pavement.
Black glass.
Statues on rooftops —
horses, swordsmen, cannon —
animated by spotlights.
Among the great buildings
the *Palacio Real,*
an ice palace,
home to the ghosts
of kings and queens
idle in life,
restless in death.

11/15

In the Velasquez gallery,
Las Meninas,
in which a tiny princess,
surrounded by misfits,
is bathed in golden light.
The king and queen are reflected
in a mirror misted with breath.
Whose breath?
And the painter himself,
rendering the scene from within,
gazes out at generations

of strangers not yet born —
the shadows of shadows,
as real to him as the dead.

11/17

On the Calle de Reina,
where all the cats are white,
a man is spearing sashimi with a fork,
twirling the blue seaweed like spaghetti.
He claims to be an encyclopedist
of the lost history —
aborted revolutions, quashed conspiracies,
failed assassinations —
preserved in documents
dating back eight centuries
to which he alone has access.

11/19

Streets alternately named after saints and sinners
and a single Street of Angels,
unmarked, unmapped,
with barred windows
padlocked doors
and a wall where the graffiti draws itself.

11/24

The old woman's dream:
a violin, a thimble, half a picture frame,
and constellations in the South Seas
known only to sailors.

12/1

Icy rain.
Church bells where there is no church.
The long streets.
No one.

12/17

I crossed paths with a woman
who gave me the name
of a place where people
can only speak in short sentences.
Meet me there, she says.

5/26/2014

Tonight I found this notebook
misplaced on a high shelf
six years ago,
wedged between old editions
of Strabo's *Geography*
and the *Poems of Meng Chiao.*
In the latter when I was twenty-two

I marked this line,

composed in the ninth century:

The traveller's heart is a flag a hundred feet high in the wind.

AN ICON OF SAINT CHRISTOPHER
ON THE ISLAND OF SYROS

Here in his church he is tattooed
with stars and robed in gold.
Rainwater pours from his sleeves.
He wades across a crystal river
with the infant Jesus on his back.

A pregnant widow kneels at the altar.
A soldier on crutches lights a candle.
The blind girl cradles her ailing cat
and lifts her eyes to the ceiling mural —
seraphs sailing by on golden clouds —

assuring herself that one day
they will rain down their blessings:
her cat will be healed, her vision restored,
and the saint, scaling the riverbank,
will beckon her to follow.

A NOVEL IN TEN CHAPTERS

1

On Christmas Day, 1957, two inmates of the state prison in Concord, New Hampshire, escaped across a frozen lake and plunged into the forest, pursued by dogs.

2

No one in that town had ever seen a more beautiful woman. Married three times, she lived alone for years and was last seen — young again — boarding a train with a small suitcase.

3

The crooked lawyer who shot himself wrote a suicide note with his left hand, though he was right-handed.

4

The moon rose behind a ship gliding through mountainous waves, the passengers on deck wearing thick coats to conceal the radiance of their bodies.

5

Her brooch was a yellow star, reflected in the still water as she recounted the story of her life.

6

Just as the engineer had designed it years ago, no one could cast a shadow while crossing the bridge into town.

7

Two blue fish hovered below the ice in the lake, their gills fluttering once every hour.

8

No one understood better than the doctor's widow that every man's life is a blind alley.

9

For the burglar's children, the prospect of another week alone was less frightening than the sight of their mother's photograph torn up, taped back together, and tacked to the wall.

10

At his funeral a blind woman sang into the rain. Dogs were approaching from the forest. The sole mourners were two old men in blue suits, shoulder to shoulder with bowed heads and laughing eyes.

FROM THE *S.S. MORAVIA* RUN AGROUND OFF KAHALA POINT

You possess only whatever will not be lost in a shipwreck.
—El-Ghazali

Nights when the moon clears the mountains
and breaks through the clouds streaming seaward
the drowned and their baggage
can still be seen tumbling in the waves.
Women with billowing dresses, sailors in white.
A jumble of hats, shoes, and broken oars.
Then the cargo of ironwood and teak,
bales of hemp and casks of ambergris.
Goats and pigs in shattered pens.
A phalanx of Dutch rats that nearly reached shore.
And the two red cats, Abyssians, that did —
the lone survivors —
poised on a crate of Sumatran cloves.
Their feral descendants still prowl the underbrush,
fur clove-scented,
eyes ocean-blue.

MIDNIGHT

At the twelfth gate of the ruined temple
a lion has crumbled into sand

The bells of a dozen churches
toll across the island

The wind whirls white petals
down the twelve alleys to the harbor

Last year twelve children were born
here and twelve people died

Below the seawall barefoot in her marble dress
a girl lost at sea for twelve days

climbs the twelve steps to the plaza
where the Angel of Tears

weeps into a fountain adorned
with the signs of the zodiac

and twelve pilgrims clutching candles
file up the mountain road

GOLDEN APPLES

They crop up in high dramas —
Hercules' eleventh labor
the Judgment of Paris —
but what the Greeks called apples
were in fact oranges

said to shine like lanterns
by the sailors who brought
them from India
to trade for gold
until the fruit lost its currency

and over time became
a party favor
a historical relic
a rare condiment
and finally (by default)

a common food
quartered and sprinkled with salt
and best eaten
before dawn
when it glows

AT THE END OF THAT LONG WINTER

which stretched into July
all the cellars in Europe
filled with blood
burning airplanes
queued for takeoff
abandoned ships ran aground
while a nurse in Belgrade
and a soldier in Madrid
dreamed the same dream
of Jupiter's moons
mountains sixty miles high
oceans of gasoline
hurricanes whirling
at the speed of sound

Today the remains
of a film poster
from that time
surfaced on the mottled wall
of a gutted building —
the title *Death Cruise*
traced in smoke

above a girl in red
leaning against a palm
her fishhook earrings
baited with roses
her jet hair whitening
before our eyes

GREEN STAR

1.

Knowing stars are sparks off the anvil of heaven
and starfish the stars that fall to sea

we should not be surprised after sipping
wine pressed from sea grapes

to see the cat's blue eyes turn green
when he perches on the girl's shoulder

and gazes through the skylight at Scorpius
where Antares the red star looms

beside the only green star known to man
Vespertilio

2.

While the name
Green Star
has been conferred on
ocean liners
airplanes
& guided missiles

motor oils

condoms

& colognes

comic strips

wine bars

& cable cars

please note

that the ancient astronomers

who described Antares

as green were correct:

when interstellar winds

(of which they knew nothing)

sweep across it

the red star Antares

reflects the pigment

of its green twin

unique in our galaxy

Vespertilio

THE HOUSE ON THE MARBLE CLIFF

1.

At 8 P.M. the table
on the marble terrace
was set for one:
cold meat black bread
a marble goblet
brimming with smoke

2.

Everything was marble:
walls and floors
bookshelves and books
even the breakers
veined black and white
shattering against the reefs below

3.

The former president-for-life
lived here under house arrest
with a cook and a sentry
who scoured the beach
for fossils from the dawn
of the Ice Age

when enormous reptiles
washed up beneath a green sun

4.

Mornings he leafed through
his stamp album in the garden —
countless images of himself
heroically depicted
as burning clouds drifted
northward from the capital
where men were once afraid
to speak his name

5.

He met his wife there
rounding a corner in the rain
and forty years later
watched her disappear
around that same corner
her hair dripping
a stray dog at her heels

6.

After he died in his bath
the cook and the sentry
laid him out on his bed
a marble slab with a thin mattress

until the soldiers sent
by his successor buried
him in an unmarked grave

7.

From the cook's deposition:
At 5 a.m. I served him coffee
at midnight milk...
I was the last person
to whom he could give orders
always in writing
never once in ten years
did he address me by name
or offer a word of thanks

8.

The state media devoted a week
to cataloging his crimes
from the petty to the unspeakable
after which he was never
mentioned again

9.

Before demolishing the house
the workmen blew open
his safe but found
no cash or jewels

just a broken watch
a bent key
and a cyanide pill
blue as the sky
wrapped in blue silk

TWO STORIES THE BLIND MAN TOLD

1

The woman who had lost her way placed the jar on the table. The lid was sealed with green wax. A lightning bolt was painted on the side. She cut the seal and pried open the lid. Wind rushed through the house. Thunder rumbled in the cellar.

Someone uncorked a bottle in the kitchen. Oil sizzled in a skillet, and the smoke of onions and sweetmeats drifted down the hall. The woman grew drowsy, overcome with dread. She closed the jar and the thunder faded.

On the road that wound past the house, cattle were bellowing, jostling, on their way to slaughter. Whips cracked over their backs. The lights in the house went out. The woman wanted to leave, but instead curled up on the floor, covering her ears.

Out in the world, across oceans and deserts, a cry went up. Cities caught fire. Rivers rose. Entire populations embraced sleep, knowing they would not awaken. The tongues of rulers and beggars alike fell silent, and the prophets became as children, busying themselves in corners, hearing nothing, saying nothing, their toys clinking in the darkness.

The contralto in the back row sprouted wings through her burgundy robe. A silver barrette shone in her hair.

She scanned the statues of angels that lined the mezzanine. Their marble robes were translucent, thin as silk. Their haloes were silver.

Mist hung in the rafters. Snowflakes stuck to the windows. A fat man on the aisle mopped his brow. A woman in green taffeta crumpled her program.

The concluding chorus was sung allegro spiritoso. The audience shivered as the second violins veered off, the oboes following them, then the cembalo, played with flying fingers by a red-haired boy.

When the final note sounded, the contralto extended her wings. All eyes turned upward as she flew through the skylight, into the clouds, emanating brilliant rays. Only when the cathedral had emptied did she return and take her place in the mezzanine, her barrette a halo now and a smile on her lips.

2

14 RUE SERPENTINE

1.

The track at the velodrome is banked
like the rings of Saturn spinning
with riders who blur away
like those fast-motion films
of flowers blossoming and dying
or of the moon in a roiled sky
sailing through its phases
Tonight the moon rises above rooftops and bridges
spreading its sea of silver light
stilling vast crowds
and for an instant reflected whole
in the spectacles of a blind man
sitting alone in a parked car

2.

In the yard of the children's prison
the fruit on the solitary tree is blue
shriveled beyond recognition
At the turn of the last century
the inmates (aged 7 to 13)
pickpockets petty thieves and vandals
ate gruel from tin bowls and slept on iron cots
gazing down from their cells
at the tree when it blossomed in April
and in September bore fruit
which the guards pocketed rocking
on their heels into the long afternoons
It was an apple tree

3.

At dusk rain slants in from the north
black needles clotting
the locomotive's cyclops beam
the prison searchlight
the streetlamp's cone
beneath which vagrants line their boots
with road maps before closing their eyes
and entering a maze of blind alleys
searching for the one doorway among thousands
that will lead away from their nightmares
and the one in a million
(where the rain dissolves into light)
that opens onto paradise

4.

Tattooed on my shoulder
a fish with golden scales
silver fins and a ruby eye
a creature last seen
three millennia ago
near the Nile delta
reputed to have entrails of pearls
coveted by the fishermen
who lined the riverbank
and waded into the reeds
shoulder to shoulder netting the fish
and gutting it for treasure not flesh
until it was rendered extinct

5.

In the Egyptian Department at the Louvre I wonder:
if the priests of the XIIth Dynasty were correct
and our dreams are memories of past lives
shattered and rearranged by the gods
if the truth is camouflaged
in the token correspondences of this world
names dates places that can be linked with ease
by even a minor deity
then the inscrutable mysteries which have tormented
me and my tormentors ought to come clear
so simple suddenly:
Happiness awaits all of us
but few find their way to her

6.

The owl no bigger than my fist
speckled blue and black
is hooting in the courtyard at dawn
when I open a letter from a friend
grieving for his daughter
quoting Martial who mourned the death
of another child two centuries ago
Earth, lie not heavy on her who walked so lightly on you
Sometimes it's not hours but years that pass in a single day
and when darkness falls again
drawing me into its circle
will I hear that same owl
or will another be perched in its place?

7.

The music that breaks into my sleep
like the wind whirring
across the Venetian lagoon
the night I crossed
the long wooden bridge
that connects Burano and Mazzorbo
identical to the bridge a psychic
drew for me in a nightclub in Prague
spanning (she said) the twin shores
of birth and death
their reefs invisible to all men
their deep currents liable to divert me
for an eternity

8.

So the dead are among us again
even here where Halloween is not celebrated
and the moon flies through the skeletons of trees
and men in rowboats fish for souls on the river
A woman with spidery hair swings a lantern
and disappears down the colonnade
past a row of buildings tilted like gravestones
in which a single window is lit
and a wall from whose depths shadows emerge
assuming the contours of bodies they will follow
all night and abandon at dawn:
a revelation to me
that each day we take on a new shadow

9.

A friend of a friend chops and sautées
morel mushrooms leeks and celery root
punctuating the narrative of her life's journey
with Sufi epigrams such as
The candle is not there to illuminate itself
Deft with a knife and light on her feet
she decants a Sauterne and declares
that she only cooks for strangers
food unlike love tenderness or true passion
so easy to give so readily received
For most men she says the more elaborate
the meal the greater the illusion of fulfillment whereas
If you are entertaining a dervish, dry bread is enough

10.

In the triangular park with the sundial
the war veteran sells his medals
a beggar plays her accordion
for the poodle dancing on its hind legs
and children line up to buy ices
persimmon apricot grenadine
from an old woman with a parrot on her shoulder
that asks the children their names
until the woman closes up her cart
and walks home rewarding the parrot
with grapes as he repeats the names
in the order he learned them
Therése Barthélemy Clarisse Victor Marie...

11.

The snake charmer's daughter
born in a carnival tent
with a crescent of stars on her brow
calls herself the Serpent Priestess
and opens a studio next door
Behind a velvet curtain her assistant
plays his flute while she shuffles tarot cards
explaining that this street was named
not for its sinuous path but for the snakes
Napoleon's soldiers brought back from Egypt
which infest the neighborhood
though I have only seen one:
the cobra coiled in a basket at her feet

12.

I dip my rotting oars
into the brown waters of the lake
and row toward the floating temple
Splinters of light escape its shuttered windows
a red lantern sways on the dock
a candle flutters by the door
I can hear the faintest sound:
fruit falling in the orchard
a snake shedding its skin in the reeds
My breathing is shallow
my hands one with the darkness
and when finally I reach the temple
my oars are gone

13.

I cross the hall with a parched throat
passing a mirror that remains blank
a birdcage with an open door
and an orrery of the solar system —
the planets and their moons
orbiting a wooden sun
The water I drink is so cold
it could have been drawn from the iceberg
the size of Delaware
that recently broke away from Antarctica —
your destination perhaps
a small voice whispers
the next time you get out of bed

14.

This is a street of widows I say
my cheeks flushed with fever
poinsettias blazing in windows
and red leaves skittering
past the house on the corner
where the Mexican painter shot himself
his grave shadowed by a steeple
in which cardinals nest
while across from the cemetery a vendor
in a scarlet apron
hands me a bag of cold cherries
shaking his head observing
No not widows this is the street of snakes

15.

An ancient messenger in a modern uniform
bicycles down the street
with a dead letter to deliver
The lines in his palm are twisted into a noose
the coins in his pocket
embossed with the visages
of corrupt kings and queens
descendants of Justinian
codifier of laws he himself broke
and Theodora his empress
who allowed panthers to roam her bedroom
and slept with teams of wrestlers
only to have them beheaded at dawn

16.

In this room where a single ray of light
penetrates the vine-covered window
the green curtain that parts
onto the circular garden
I dip my hands into a basin of water
and they blur away
only the lines from my upturned palms remain
floating for an instant
realigning themselves
then disappearing
a map to guide me for the rest of my life
or until I leave this address
whichever comes first

17.

Returning to the cool galleries
of the museum as sunlight pours
through the windows I admire
the bronze statue of Queen Karomana
the ivory-handled knife of Gebelel-Arak
and the stela of King Djet (the Serpent King)
Then I take a train from the Gare de Lyon
to Pontoise where fishermen in black capes
net eels in the swollen river
and during the return trip dream of jackals
shrouded in mist circling the Valley of the Kings
their howls across thousands of miles
waking me in a sweat

18.

A city in Central Asia
a square walled in by granite buildings
bits of paper rising twenty stories on the wind
the two walkways that form an X
choked with weeds
at its center a cement Buddha
with a forehead cracked by the cold
From a rooftop a woman in green
calls repeatedly to a child
whose name I would like
to tell her is scrawled
in crayon beneath a face —
closed eyes and a downturned mouth —
on a door I'm about to open

19.

Electric-green palms
tom-toms in the mountains
birds iridescent as the clouds at dawn:
I was on a crescent beach
beneath a vast sky
at some juncture in another life
trying to find my way
until I realized
I must not move for once —
not when rain pelted my skin
or bees stung
not when the ghost of a butterfly brushed my arm
That was all I needed to know

20.

You need not read the *Annals* of Tacitus

or his contemporary Sima Qian in Yunan

to know we will never refrain

from doing unto others

before they can do unto us

and therefore have invented gods

to bestow their blessings

and incite conflagrations

that must destroy us all

earthly agents and true believers praying

despite centuries of unanswered prayers

that we might still salvage

a measure of grace and mercy

and lifting our blindfolds step from the darkness

21.

On the street upturned for an instant
the face of a Siamese princess
a Mayan dancer cross-legged on a bench
Phoenician twins playing flutes beneath a cypress
the populations of lost places still among us
until at nightfall they dissolve in the mist
or assume the forms of animals
to be glimpsed sidelong
a tail a wing a transparent eyelid
just as strangers attempt from passing
impressions to imagine us whole
placing us outside of time:
as immortal as we'll ever get

NOTES

p. 32

The line that concludes the poem was written in the ninth century, at the end of his life, by Po Chü-i. It concerns a dream in which the poet finds all of his old friends who have died and asks himself, "Among the shadows of the Terrace of Night did you know them or not?" [Translation by Arthur Waley]

p. 41

The "golden apples" of the ancient Greeks were indeed oranges. The fruit originated in China and made its way west to the Mediterranean. It was with oranges that Melanion distracted Atalanta in their famous footrace. Hercules stole three oranges from the Garden of the Hesperides. Hesiod, Pausanias, Apollonius of Rhodes, Apollodorus, Diodorus Siculus, and in our own time, John McPhee, are among the authors who report that oranges were the favorite fruit of the gods.

p. 60

Martial, *Epigrammas,* V 34. The translation is my own.

p. 63

The Sufi epigrams are from *The Way of the Sufi,* by Idries Shah; Arkana/ Penguin, New York. 1990

p. 69

The Empress Theodora's depravity is chronicled by the sixth century Byzantine historian Procopius in *The Secret History*. As a high government official — he was at one time Prefect of Byzantium — Procopius had close, and obviously intimate, knowledge of Justinian's court.

ACKNOWLEDGMENTS

Poems in this book previously appeared in the following publications:

Granta	"On Jupiter Place"
The New Yorker	"The Graveyard Shift"
Little Star	"The Secret Life of Lois Lane"
TriQuarterly	"14 rue Serpentine," #s 6, 15, 17, 18
Ploughshares	"14 rue Serpentine," #s 2, 10, 12, 20
Georgia Review	"14 rue Serpentine," #s 1, 5, 8, 9, 21
Northwest Review	"Two Stories the Blind Man Told"

ABOUT THE AUTHOR

Nicholas Christopher is the author of seventeen books: eight previous volumes of poetry, most recently, *Crossing the Equator: New & Selected Poems*; six novels, including *The Soloist*, *Veronica*, and *A Trip to the Stars*; a nonfiction book, *Somewhere in the Night: Film Noir & the American City*; and a novel for children, *The True Adventures of Nicolò Zen*. He lives in New York City.

Printed in the United States
by Baker & Taylor Publisher Services